Justine and Joey
AT THE ZOO

A Zoo Yoga Book for Kids

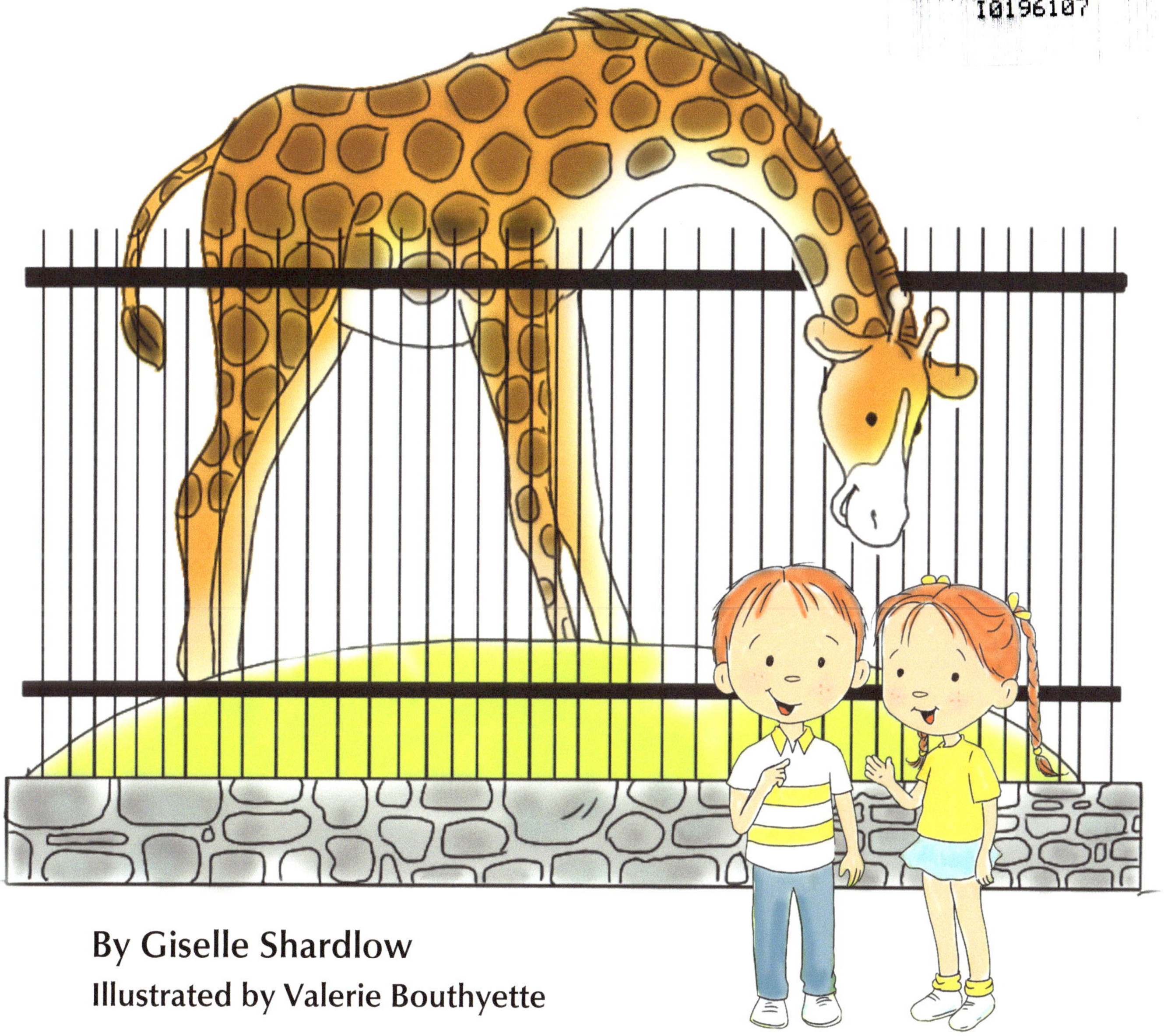

By Giselle Shardlow

Illustrated by Valerie Bouthyette

www.kidsyogastories.com

Copyright © 2018 by Giselle Shardlow
Cover and illustrations by Valerie Bouthyette
All images © 2018 Giselle Shardlow

All rights reserved. No part of this book may be reproduced in any form by any electronic or mechanical means, including photocopying, recording, or information storage and retrieval without written permission from the author. The author, illustrator, and publisher accept no responsibility or liability for any injuries or losses that may result from practicing the yoga poses outlined in this storybook. Please ensure your own safety and the safety of the children.

ISBN-13: 978-1-943648-24-5
ISBN-10: 1-943648-24-7

Kids Yoga Stories
Boston, MA
www.kidsyogastories.com
www.amazon.com/author/giselleshardlow

Email us at info@kidsyogastories.com

Ordering Information: Special discounts are available on quantity purchases by contacting the publisher at the email address above.

What do you think? Let us know what you think of *Justine and Joey at the Zoo* at feedback@kidsyogastories.com.

Printed in the United States of America.

How to Use this Yoga Book for Kids

Welcome to Kids Yoga Stories. Our yoga books are designed to integrate learning, movement, mindfulness, and fun. Below are a few tips for getting the most out of this zoo yoga book:

1. **Flip** through the story to familiarize yourself with the format. Pay special attention to the yoga pose in the circle on each page. Each pose has a corresponding keyword.

2. **Read** the story with your child, but this time, act out the story as you go along. Use the illustrations of Justine and Joey practicing the poses as a guide. Encourage your child's imagination.

3. **Refer** to the list of yoga poses for kids and the parent-teacher guide at the back of the book for further information.

Enjoy your yoga story, but please be safe!

"We're here! Hooray! I love animals!"

Justine skips down the path
while her brother, Joey, quietly studies the zoo guide.

She spots some kangaroos and wallabies.

"Yoo-hoo! Over here!" Justine yells.

The animals just stare.

"Come on, Justine.
The bird show is about to start!"
Joey says.

"Cool! Let's go!"
Justine races toward the stage.
She finds two seats in the front row.

During the show, the bird keeper asks for volunteers.

Joey raises his hand.

When a bird lands on him, he stands perfectly still, smiling.

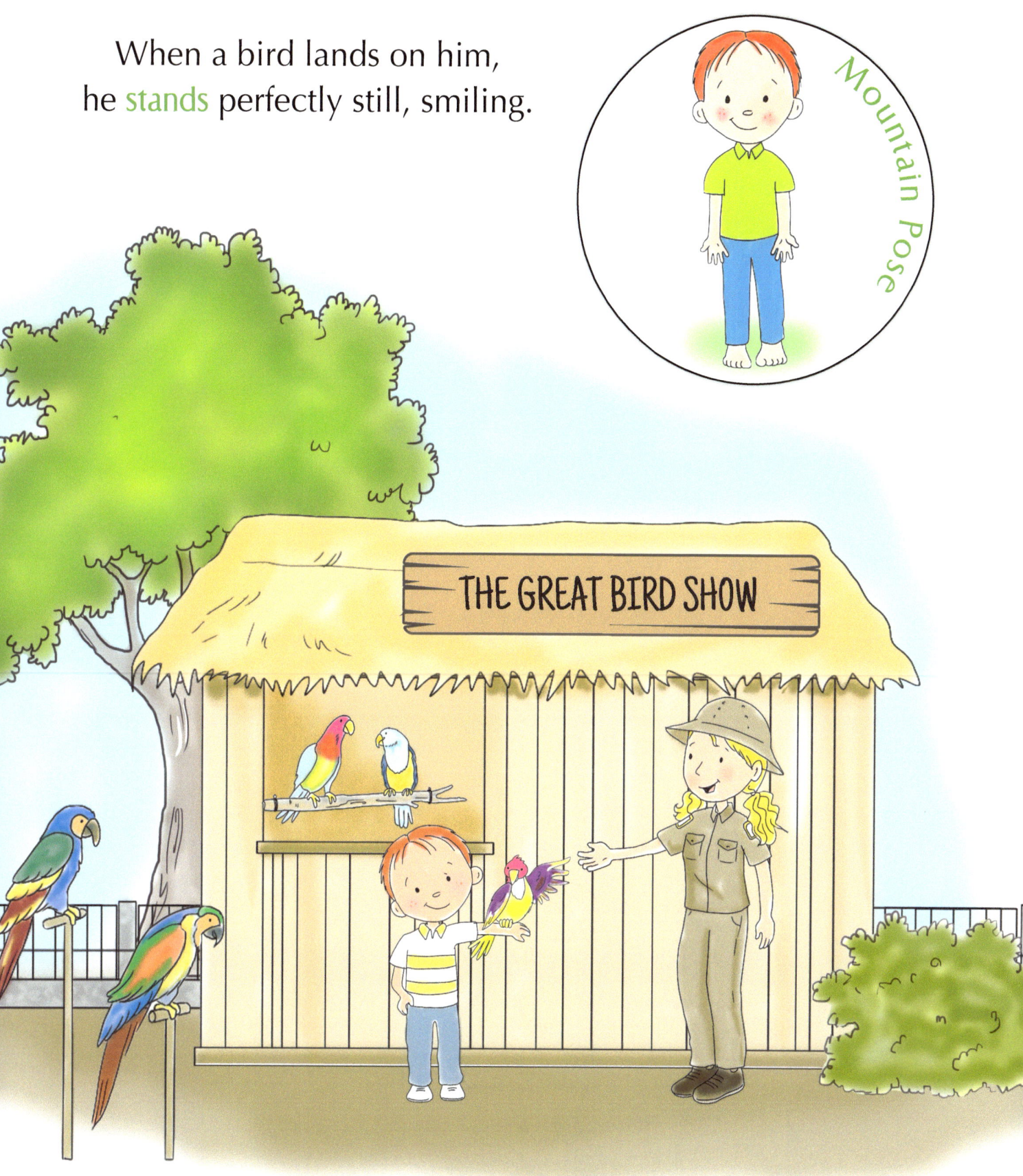

When Joey returns to his seat, Justine asks, "How did you get that bird to land on you, Joey?"

"I imagined being still and quiet in the forest," Joey says.

Justine doesn't hear him, though.

She's already heading toward the chimpanzee enclosure.

Justine jumps up and down,
trying to get the chimpanzees to do tricks.
The chimpanzees start to jump up and down, too.
Then they yelp loudly.

"Justine, let's be still for a bit," Joey says,
gently touching his sister's shoulder.
"The chimpanzees seem like they're getting upset."

"Oh, all right! I'll try doing it your way, Joey."

Justine and Joey stand in silence for a few moments.

Joey takes in a deep breath.

To their surprise, a baby chimpanzee approaches and makes eye contact with Justine.

"Wow, did you see that, Joey?" Justine whispers. "That baby chimpanzee came over to talk to me!"

Joey smiles with pride.
Now that his sister has calmed down,
she's connecting with the animals.

"Look! Tigers are next on the map," Joey says.

When Justine and Joey get there, the male tiger is pacing back and forth.

"Let's try this again, Justine. Come stand here quietly, and let's see if the tiger notices us," Joey says.

Sure enough, the tiger walks over and tilts his head. He looks curious.

Justine grabs Joey's hand tightly.

"Take a deep breath, Justine.
It'll help you feel less scared."

The tiger continues to look at them.

"Don't forget there's a fence between us,"
Joey reminds his sister. "The tiger can't hurt us."

Mindful Breathing

The pair are as still as statues until the tiger finally wanders off.

"I did it!" Justine says, giving her brother a huge hug.

As they walk to the camel ride, Joey says, "See, Justy? There's no reason to hurry. Let's go slow and enjoy the animals."

They line up together to ride the camel.

When it's her turn, Justine strokes the camel's neck.

"Feel how soft the camel is, Joey."

She takes his hand and places it on the camel's back.

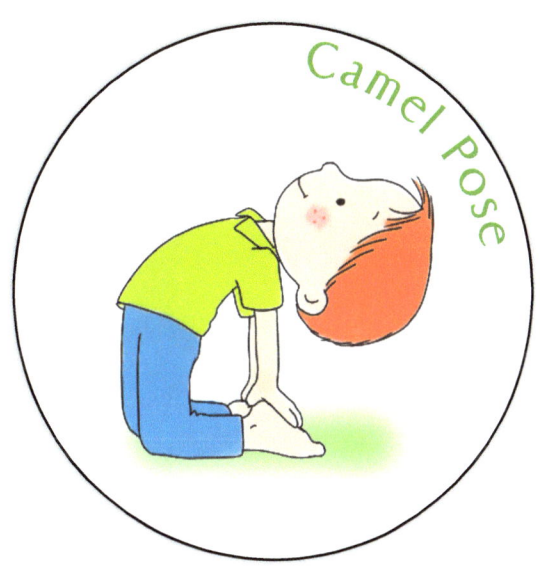

After the camel ride, Joey looks at the guide again.
"The train ride is just down this path.
We'll get to see some forest animals."

The train engineer points out the elk, eagle, and egret.

"Close your eyes and feel that warm breeze on your face," Joey says as he lets out a big sigh.

Staff Pose

"Can we feed the deer now?"
Justine asks as the train rolls to a stop.

"Great idea!" Joey replies.

They follow a path to the large fenced-off area where the white-tailed deer live.

At first, the deer run away and hide behind the trees.

"Just hold out your hand with the food. Maybe the deer will come to us," Justine says.

A few minutes later, three small deer timidly eat from their hands.

Joey is mesmerized by the experience. He's never been so close to a deer before. "This is magic, Justy!"

As they leave the deer enclosure,
Justine points to an ice cream stand.

"I'm getting mint chip!" she declares.

"Chocolate for me!" says Joey.

Reverse Plank Pose

After their snack,
they head over to the playground.

"Joey, you're right,"
Justine says from the top of the slide.
"It's more fun to go slow
and enjoy the zoo."

"My yoga teacher told us,
'Wherever you are, be there.'
He said that sometimes
our bodies are somewhere,
but our minds are somewhere else,
thinking of other things.
I've been practicing being in the present
and focusing on where I am.
And I wonder if the animals
somehow know that, too."

After the playground,
they visit the giraffes.

A zookeeper is there
with a bucket of carrots.

"Could we help feed them?" Justine asks.

The zookeeper calls one of the giraffes over.

"I'm imagining being on a safari,"
Justine says softly as a giraffe grabs a carrot from her.

Joey can't believe how calm Justine is being
when she's so close to the giraffe.
He's proud that his sister is finally in tune with the animals.

On their way to the exit, they pass a slow-moving tortoise, and Justine giggles.

"I'm going to pretend to be a tortoise.
I'm going to slow down and enjoy my life.
It's fun!"

"I'm tired," Joey says.
"Let's go lie down and rest like the kangaroos."

Joey and Justine lie on the grass together, looking up at the sky.

"Thanks for your help today, Joey.
You're the best brother in the world."

Resting Pose

List of Yoga Poses for Kids

	Keyword	Yoga Pose	Demonstration
1	Kangaroo	Chair Pose	
2	Stands	Mountain Pose	
3	Bird	Warrior 3 Pose	
4	Jumps Up and Down	Star Jumps	
5	Chimpanzee	Squat Pose	
6	Tiger	Extended Cat Pose	
7	Deep Breath	Hero Pose and Mindful Breathing	

	Keyword	Yoga Pose	Demonstration
8	Camel	Camel Pose	
9	Train	Staff Pose	
10	Deer	Seated Twist	
11	Slide	Reverse Plank Pose	
12	Giraffe	Legs Up the Wall Pose	
13	Tortoise	Tortoise Pose	
14	Lie Down	Resting Pose	

How to Practice the Yoga Poses

The following list is intended as a guide only. Please encourage the children's creativity while ensuring their safety.

Chair Pose
Stand tall in Mountain Pose with your feet hip-width apart, bend your knees, and keep a straight spine. Hold your hands out in front of you, pretending to be a kangaroo.

Mountain Pose
Stand tall with your legs hip-width apart and feet facing forward. Take your arms out straight alongside your body and imagine a bird landing on your shoulder.

Warrior 3 Pose
Stand on one leg. Extend the other leg behind you, flexing your foot. Bend your torso forward and take your arms back alongside your body. Pretend you are a parrot flying through the air.

Star Jumps
Start in Mountain Pose with your feet hip-width distance apart. Then bend your knees and jump up as high as you can while splaying out your legs. Do a few rounds of star jumps to release any pent-up energy.

Squat Pose
Come down to a squat with your knees apart and your arms between your knees. Pretend to be a baby chimpanzee sitting on a rock.

Extended Cat Pose

Come to all fours, extend one leg out behind you, and look forward. Take the opposite arm out in front of you to counter balance. Pretend to be a tiger dashing across its enclosure. Repeat on the other side.

Hero Pose with Mindful Breathing

Come to rest upright on your heels with your palms resting on your knees. Start a three-count inhale, followed by a three-count exhale to practice mindful breathing. Imagine standing by the fence with a tiger on the other side and mindfully releasing your fear.

Camel Pose

Come to a kneeling position, with your toes either curled under or flat on the ground. Lift your head, open your chest, squeeze your shoulders, and place your palms on your buttocks. Gently take your hips forward while shifting your shoulders back, slowly arching your back. If comfortable, take your hands to your heels and relax your head. Imagine being a camel at the zoo.

Staff Pose

Sit with a tall spine with your legs straight out in front of you. Move your hands like the wheels of a train going down the track at the zoo.

Seated Twist

Start by sitting cross-legged. Bend your right knee and place your right foot behind your left knee. Check that your spine is straight and your right foot is flat on the ground. Twist your upper body to the right. Take your left elbow to your right knee and your right hand back behind you. Pretend to be a deer sitting in a meadow. Repeat on the other side.

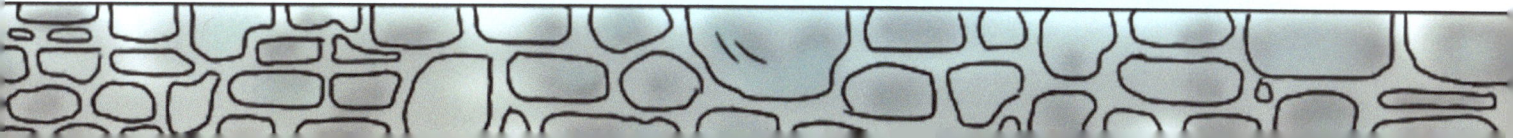

Reverse Plank Pose

From Staff Pose, place your palms flat behind you and open your chest. Lift your buttocks to a reverse plank position with your legs and spine straight and feet flat on the ground. Pretend you are a playground slide from your head to your toes.

Legs Up the Wall Pose

Lie flat on your back then slowly raise your legs straight up toward the sky, making an L shape with your body. Keeping your legs together, flex your feet. Spread your arms out to either side and keep your neck in a neutral position. You could also rest your legs up a wall instead. Pretend that your legs are the long neck of a giraffe.

Tortoise Pose

Sit on your buttocks with your knees bent and your feet flat on the floor. Then take your feet out wide and be sure you are sitting with a tall, straight spine. Slide your arms under your knees and place your hands flat on the floor outside your legs. Bend forward, keeping your back and neck straight. Pretend to be a tortoise poking its head out of the shell.

Resting Pose

Lie on your back with your arms and legs stretched out. Breathe and rest. Think about your favorite part of the zoo visit.

Parent-Teacher Guide

This guide contains tips to get the most out of
your experience of yoga stories with young children.

Put safety first. Ensure that the space is clear and clean. Spend some time clearing any dangerous objects or unnecessary items. Wear comfortable clothing and practice barefoot.

Props are welcome. Yoga mats or towels (on a non-slip surface) are optional. Zoo-related props and zoo-themed music are a good addition.

Cater to the age group. Use this Kids Yoga Stories book as a guide, but make adaptations according to the age of your children. Feel free to lengthen or shorten your journey to ensure that your children are fully engaged throughout your time together. We recommend reading this book with children ages three to six (toddlers to kindergartners).

Talk together. Engage your children in the book's topic. Talk about their visits to a zoo or their favorite zoo books so they can form meaningful connections. Explain the purpose of yoga stories–to integrate movement, reading, and fun.

Learn through movement. Brain research shows that we learn best through physical activity. Our bodies are designed to be active. Encouraging your children to act out the keywords allows them to have fun while learning about the zoo. Use repetition to engage the children and help them learn the movements. Ask your child to say or predict the next pose in their pretend zoo visit.

Develop breath awareness. Throughout the practice, bring the children's attention to the action of inhaling and exhaling in a light-hearted way. For example, encourage children to stand still in silence and take a deep breath when they are watching the bird show, monkeys, and tigers.

Relax. Allow your children time to end their session in Resting Pose for five to ten minutes. Massage their feet during or after their relaxation period. Relaxation techniques give children a way to deal with stress. Reinforce the benefits and importance of quiet time for their minds and bodies. Introduce meditation, which can be as simple as sitting quietly for a couple of minutes, as a way to bring stillness to their highly stimulated lives.

Lighten up and enjoy yourself. A children's yoga experience is not as formal as an adult class. Encourage the children to use their creativity and provide them time to explore the postures. Avoid teaching perfectly aligned poses. The journey is intended to be joyful and fun. Your children feed off your passion and enthusiasm. So take the opportunity to energize yourself, as well. Read and act out the yoga book together as a way to connect with each other.

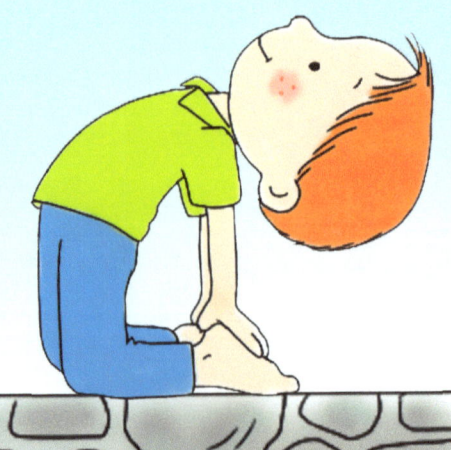

About Kids Yoga Stories

We hope you enjoyed your Kids Yoga Stories experience.

Visit www.kidsyogastories.com to:

Receive updates. For yoga tips, updates, contest giveaways, articles, and activity ideas, sign up for our free **Kids Yoga Stories Newsletter.**

Connect with us. Please share with us about your yoga journey. Send pictures of yourself practicing the poses or reading the story. Describe your journey on our social media pages (Facebook, Pinterest, Google+, Instagram, and Twitter).

Check out free stuff. Read our articles on books, yoga, parenting, and travel. Download one of our kids yoga lesson plans or coloring pages.

Read or write a review. Read what others have to say about our yoga books for kids or post your own review on Amazon or on our website. We would love to hear how you enjoyed this yoga book.

Thank you for your support in spreading our message of integrating learning, movement, and fun.

Giselle

Kids Yoga Stories
www.kidsyogastories.com
giselle@kidsyogastories.com
www.pinterest.com/kidsyogastories
www.facebook.com/kidsyogastories
www.twitter.com/kidsyogastories
www.amazon.com/author/giselleshardlow
www.goodreads.com/giselleshardlow

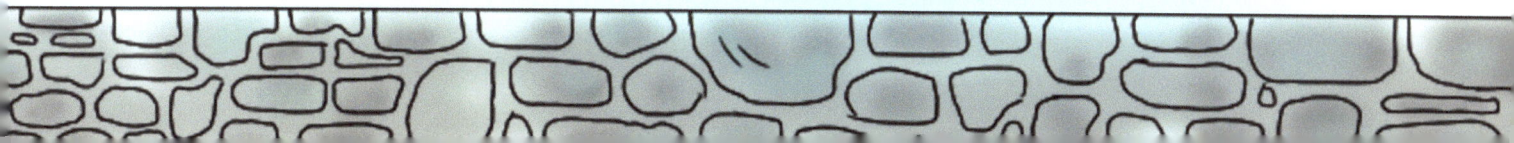

About the Author

Giselle Shardlow draws from her experiences as a teacher, traveler, mother, and yogi to write her yoga stories for children. The purpose of her yoga books is to foster happy, healthy, and globally educated children. She lives in Boston with her husband and daughter.

About the Illustrator

Valerie Bouthyette is an award-winning graphic designer and fine artist, who holds degrees in Advertising Art and Design and is an NYS Certified Early Childhood teacher. Valerie calls on her imagination and memories of childhood to create illustrations that warm your heart and make you smile. She creates in her studio nestled in the farmlands, which she refers to as "her heaven." Valerie lives with her husband in upstate NY, where they also own a small horse-boarding facility.

Other Yoga Books by Giselle Shardlow

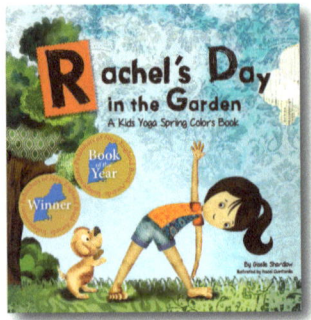
Rachel's Day in the Garden

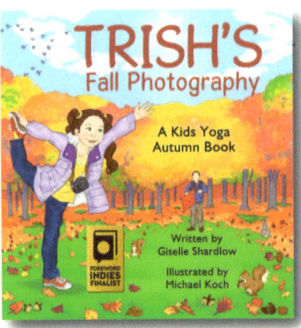
Trish's Fall Photography

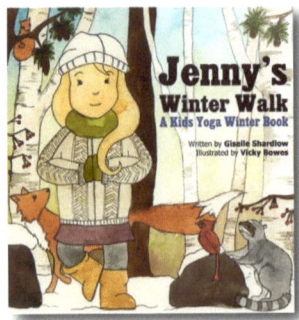
Jenny's Winter Walk

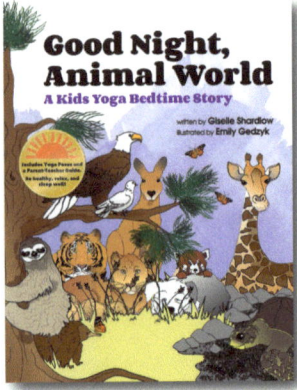
Good Night, Animal World

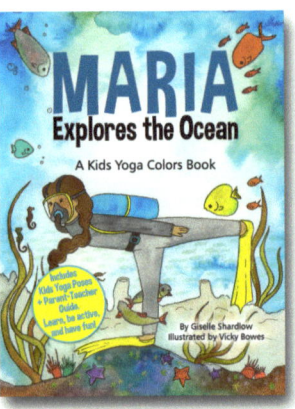
Maria Explores the Ocean

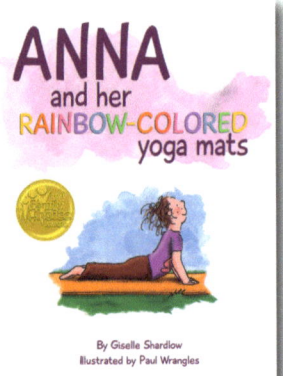
Anna and her Rainbow-Colored Yoga Mats

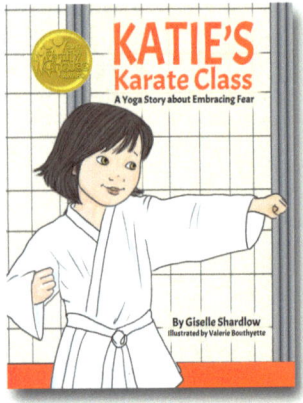
Katie's Karate Class

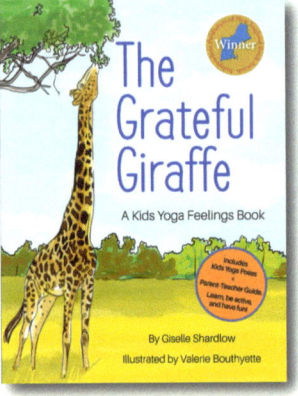
The Grateful Giraffe

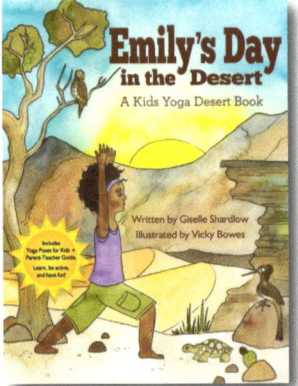
Emily's Day in the Desert

Many of the yoga books above are available in multiple languages and eBook format.

Buy your yoga books here:
www.kidsyogastories.com

www.ingramcontent.com/pod-product-compliance
Lightning Source LLC
Chambersburg PA
CBHW042123040426
42450CB00002B/53